WILD WATER

by Noah Leatherland

Minneapolis, Minnesota

Credits
Images are courtesy of Shutterstock.com. With thanks to Getty Images, Thinkstock Photo, and iStockphoto. Cover – Dmitry Naumov, olrat. Recurring – hugolacasse, donatas1205. 2–3 – Gopal3366. 4–5 – Dikushin Dmitry, Olleg Visual Content, DjelicS. 6–7 – optimarc, daniilphotos. 8–9 – Gwoeii, Rad Radu. 10–11 – bikemp, BMJ. 12–13 – Dmitry Naumov, Jonathan_Moe. 14–15 – Kat72, Elaine Davis. 16–17 – Imfoto, Damsea. 18–19 – Collin Quinn Lomax, Pecold, AzmanJaka. 20–21 – Ammit Jack, Amateur007, tdub303. 22–23 – Allexxandar, Aleksandr Lupin.

Bearport Publishing Company Product Development Team
Publisher: Jen Jenson; Director of Product Development: Spencer Brinker; Editorial Director: Allison Juda; Editor: Cole Nelson; Editor: Tiana Tran; Production Editor: Naomi Reich; Art Director: Kim Jones; Designer: Kayla Eggert; Designer: Steve Scheluchin; Production Specialist: Owen Hamlin

Library of Congress Cataloging-in-Publication Data is available at www.loc.gov or upon request from the publisher.

ISBN: 979-8-89577-082-5 (hardcover)
ISBN: 979-8-89577-529-5 (paperback)
ISBN: 979-8-89577-199-0 (ebook)

© 2026 BookLife Publishing
This edition is published by arrangement with BookLife Publishing.

North American adaptations © 2026 Bearport Publishing Company. All rights reserved. No part of this publication may be reproduced in whole or in part, stored in any retrieval system, or transmitted in any form or by any means, electronic, mechanical, photocopying, recording, or otherwise, without written permission from the publisher. Bearport Publishing is a division of FlutterBee Education Group.

For more information, write to Bearport Publishing, 3500 American Blvd W, Suite 150, Bloomington, MN 55431.

CONTENTS

Our Home 4
Wild Water. 6
Making a River 8
Rapids. 10
Whitewater. 12
Whirlpools. 14
Hidden Danger 16
Wild Water Riders. 18
Staying Safe 20
Safe Studies 22
Glossary 24
Index 24

OUR HOME

Check out our home planet, Earth! It has everything we need to live. However, not everything on Earth is very nice. . . .

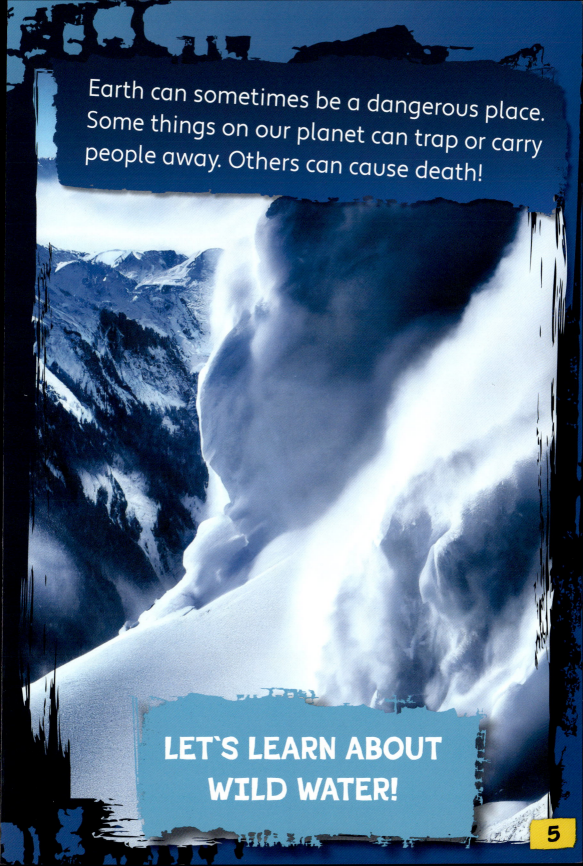

Earth can sometimes be a dangerous place. Some things on our planet can trap or carry people away. Others can cause death!

LET'S LEARN ABOUT WILD WATER!

WILD WATER

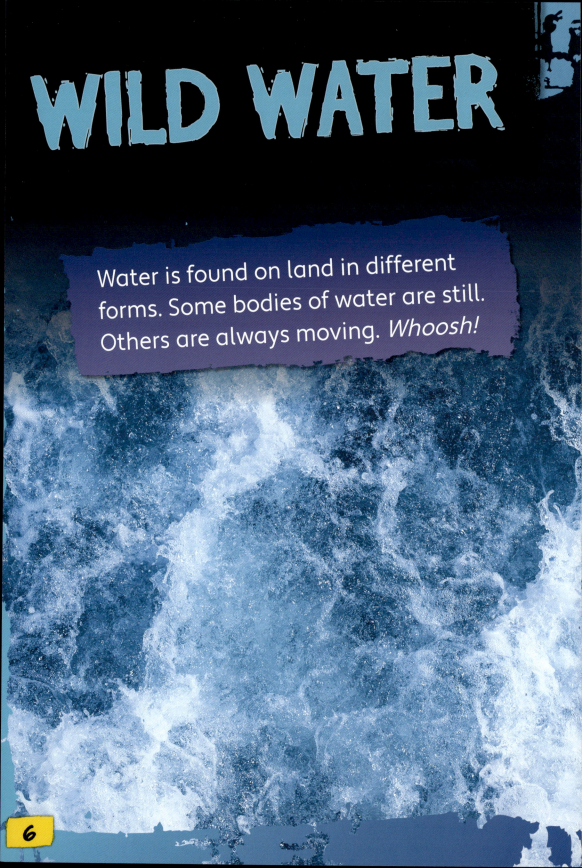

Water is found on land in different forms. Some bodies of water are still. Others are always moving. *Whoosh!*

Rivers can sometimes get rough and choppy. Their **currents** can flow fast. This makes them very dangerous.

MAKING A RIVER

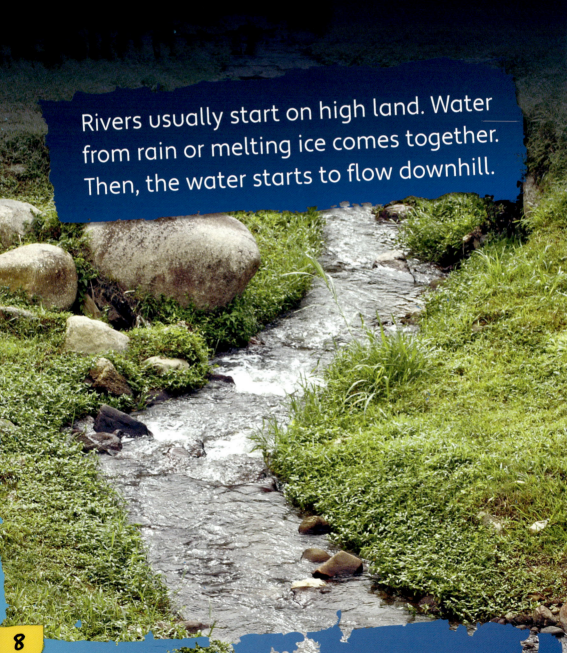

Rivers usually start on high land. Water from rain or melting ice comes together. Then, the water starts to flow downhill.

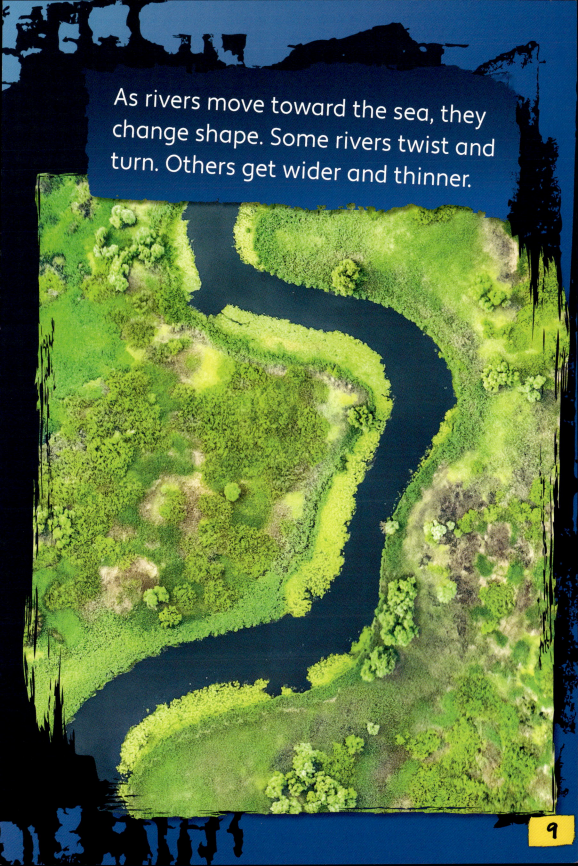

As rivers move toward the sea, they change shape. Some rivers twist and turn. Others get wider and thinner.

RAPIDS

Rapids are quick, violent stretches of water. They often form in **shallow** parts of the river. Rapids are usually **steep**.

Rapids can have small or big waves. As it moves over differently shaped rocks, the water becomes more rough.

WHITEWATER

Water splashing in rapids looks frothy and white. This is called whitewater.

Whitewater

The water looks white because it has extra air in it. This air is good for the living things in and around the river.

WHIRLPOOLS

Currents in rapids can move in different directions. When two currents come together, they form whirlpools (WURL-poolz).

A whirlpool

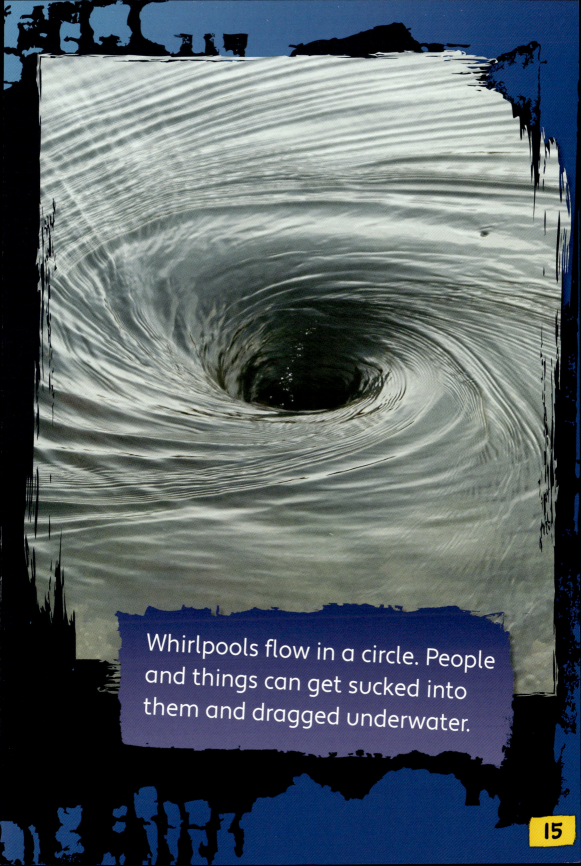

Whirlpools flow in a circle. People and things can get sucked into them and dragged underwater.

HIDDEN DANGER

Wild water may sometimes look calm. But don't be fooled! It can be hard to know what is happening under the **surface**.

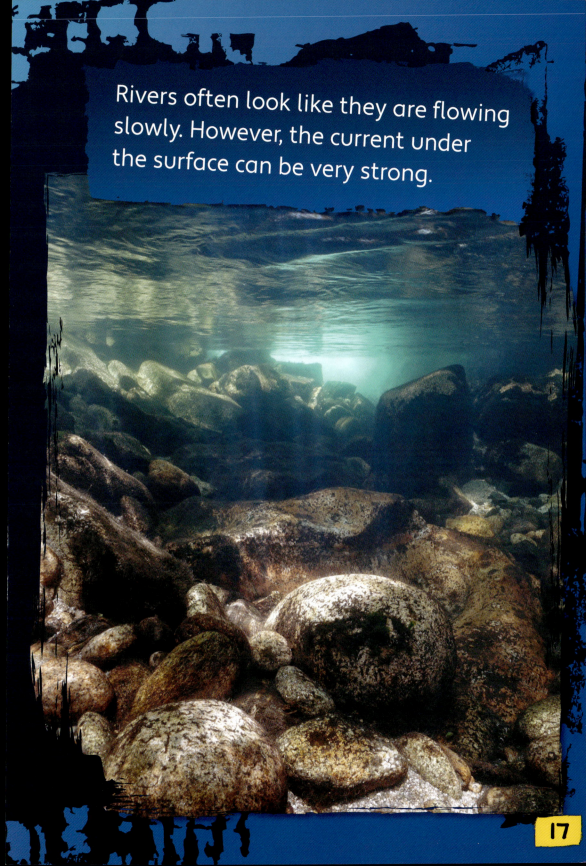

Rivers often look like they are flowing slowly. However, the current under the surface can be very strong.

WILD WATER RIDERS

Some people enjoy the thrill of riding wild waters. They make their way through the waves using kayaks, canoes, and rafts.

A kayak

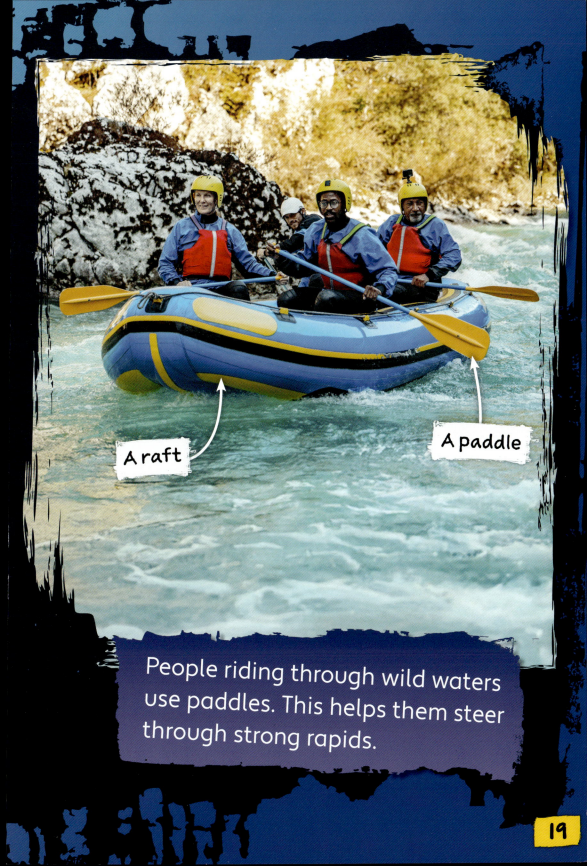

A raft

A paddle

People riding through wild waters use paddles. This helps them steer through strong rapids.

STAYING SAFE

Rapids and rivers can be dangerous. It takes more than small boats and paddles to keep wild water riders safe.

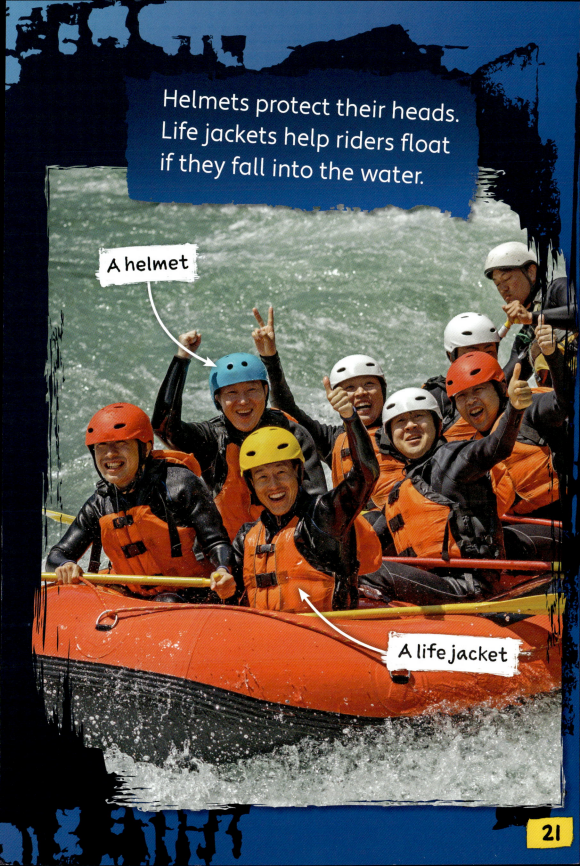

Helmets protect their heads. Life jackets help riders float if they fall into the water.

A helmet

A life jacket

SAFE STUDIES

Wild water is super interesting to learn about. However, it can be very dangerous.

Leave riding wild water to the **experts**! They know the best ways to handle the waves while staying safe.

GLOSSARY

currents movements of water from one place to another

experts people who know a lot about a subject

shallow not very deep

steep something that goes almost straight up and down

surface the top layer of something

INDEX

currents 7, 14, 17
experts 23
helmets 21
ice 8
life jackets 21
paddles 19–20

rain 8
rapids 10–12, 14, 19–20
rocks 11
sea 6, 9